Haya Berkowitz

WORDS TO PONDER N∘1

- Translated from French

ISBN: 9798589230963

Words to Ponder

Sources: All these Words are taken from the writings of the Sages of Israel

Table of Contents

1- Man doesn't control of his fate

Everyone's life is planned with good and bad events, already before he was born. The assertion of this comes from King David and Jeremiah the prophet:

"Your eyes saw me when I was a shapeless mass, and on your Book were written all the days that were reserved for me without a single one having yet hatched."

Likewise, the prophet Jeremiah received a message regarding his role in life:

"The word of the Lord came to me: 'Even before I formed you in your mother's womb, I knew you; before you come today, I consecrated you; I make you a prophet to the nations.'"

The Ramchal[1] teaches: *"All creatures depend on the Creator and they are nothing other than the result of His influence over them. That is why they are not in control of their actions."*

"Lord, I know it: man is not master of his fate; it is not given to him who walks to direct his steps. "

However, free will does exist. It is used to accept or rebel against the events of our lives and to make moral decisions.

---

[1] Rabbi Moshe Hayim Luzzatto

Why do some people choose not to do GOOD? Then, the question is: Will they get where they want to go, and in what condition?

For example, Jonah, the prophet, did not want to fulfill his mission. He was commanded by God to go to Nineveh, and bring the city's people to repent. A prophet who refuses his mission is condemned to death by his Creator. God, who is kind, gave him a test to bring him to repentance before applying the decree of death. Jonah first had to be swallowed by a fish and suffer in her stomach to be able to beg God to give him another chance. Because of this, Nineveh had to wait a little longer to see God's emissary arrive and bring them to repentance. Likewise, twelve Hebrews, among the sons of Jacob who were still encamped in the desert, wanted to explore Canaan's land before settling there with the people. They wanted to see this place with their own eyes, when God had told them that the earth there was good and that milk and honey were flowing in it. Why did ten spies see a land of Canaan which eats its inhabitants, and made the free choice not to enter it, while two spies saw a land flowing with milk and honey, discovering the same landscape? Their free will was in their thoughts and their choice.

"A man's heart chooses his way, but the Lord guides his steps."

Where man wants to go, God pushes him. Yet, the divine plan has not changed. The Hebrews will go to the land that God has chosen for them, only with a delay. The generation that does not want to submit to God will die in the desert. Their children only will enter. After this terrible decree, people changed their minds. It was too late. They couldn't go back because the moment of the decision had passed. Moses intervened on their behalf, but without effect. The ten spies, who saw the evil of the land of Canaan, died of an epidemic. However, God agreed to forgive the rest of the people who followed the ten's advice. God accepted their repentance, but it came at a price. They still had to pay for their fault. The cost to pay is calculated 'measure for measure.' God declared that they would not die immediately; but they would end their lives in the wilderness where they wanted to stay and live in eternal regret.

God asserts that his "General Plan" is dictated by his providence. However, the details of how that plan unfolds is left to man's responsibility. God is involved in our lives. We will see later how God prepares us for our role, but we are responsible for the intention of our actions and our behavior.

2- Joy does not await man

Joy does not await man.[2] He must seek it. He must force himself to be happy with what he has received from Heaven. When one acquires joy, it is like a magnet. Joy attracts human beings and, in return, makes them feel good. Therefore, man must make the necessary efforts to accept himself as born imperfect while trying to complete his lacks and weaknesses. One

---

[2] Extract from my book "Create Joy"

must strive to perfect himself and be proud of his efforts, determination, and will. It will help him to achieve joy. Then, he will be able to spread his happiness around. It's like a squirt of love because the other feels happy. However, the 'recipient' of this joy will relapse into sadness if he moves away from his giver or does not also try to become a 'giver of joy.' Those who cling to sadness, sadness clings to them like a leech and does not let go.

The need to be honored and approved by others destroys the joy of being you. Pay no attention to others' judgments that are all different from yours since each has a unique brain and unique thoughts. If you need to be approved by others, you will never have a natural and intuitive behavior, but one that is subject to please those around you; then you will feel frustrated and angry. Human, by nature, likes to belittle his neighbor. Do what is right and just, and breeds peace and unity. Rest assured that by doing that, you will strengthen your inner edifice. It will make you happy, and your Creator will approve of you. If you are satisfied with your work on yourself, and feel that God appreciates you, others will support and look for you without even seeking it.

"Serve the Lord with joy; come gladly into his presence!"[3]

In the Torah, the One God will hold us responsible if we don't serve him with joy.

---

[3] Psalm 100 ; 2

3- Live the Present

A friend from France told me that the future worries her. It prevents her from focusing on spiritual thoughts, which are not as urgent as the current situation. Know that joy is in appreciating the present moment:

"This is the day that God has made. Let us rejoice and be happy!" [4]

The saying goes that yesterday is past and tomorrow may never come, so why worry for tomorrow when we neglect

---

[4] Psalm 118.24

the present. It is in the present that we build our life, that we strengthen our inner edifice. We create our well-being by changing our negative thoughts into positive ones.

Creativity gives exceptional satisfaction. Reaching out to each other by phone or respecting social distance makes us happy. So, my dear friend, find a goal to achieve, make a schedule for your day, study something new. The old saying goes, "*Lost time can't be made up.*"

When our thoughts are lost in past times reveries or future imaginations. These times are not times of fulfillment. The present is a new day, a day when you can do yourself some good by enjoying life, accomplishing tasks, and being able to admire the beautiful things in the world.

Gratitude is the best medicine for anxiety. Count your blessings every day. Say 'thank you' to God or the universe if you prefer, and you will feel better.

"*Start a new life every moment*," teaches Rabbi Nachman of Breslev.

Live only your day. Don't ask yourself what will happen tomorrow or the day after.

4- Love is an immense force

The world has progressed phenomenally in all techniques, sciences, medicine, high tech, space, and more, but yet the lack of love words remains the same, profound, painful, and degrading. Hatred reigns among men and nations; wars, violence, aggressions prove it. As a human being, you have to be afraid of wasting your life; you have to be fearful of destroying yourself for lack of love; that is, lack of self-love, lack of love of others, and lack of love of God.

"The only reason we're on earth is to learn to love," wrote Thornton Wilder.

"Love your neighbor as yourself."[5]

This is the whole Torah. It must be remembered that man's neighbor was given the same structure as him: the good inclination and the evil inclination. Therefore, we must look for positive points in ourselves and others, teaches Rabbi Nachman, and surely erase the hatred. Likewise, if I forgive my neighbor, I do myself good because the hatred gnaws at the man inside.

Hate spares no one, Jews or non-Jews, believers or unbelievers. This negative emotion must be immediately controlled and rejected. Wars, with their

---

[5] Leviticus 19 ;18

millions of dead, are an example of pride and gratuitous hatred.

The ultimate human fear is to wake up and not know how well you have managed your life. This worry should help you decide to love. He, who knows how to love, succeeds. Love is a work, a goal that requires daily efforts: Do not judge others unless you are in their shoes, do not sully or defame another human being without constructive reasons, and do not misbehave to save your life.

The Baal Shem Tov said, "*Your happiness in life depends on the quality of your thoughts.*" So even in confinement, we can do *teshuva*[6] on our errors and weaknesses not yet repaired.

---

[6] Repent and return to God

Bayha Ibn Pakuda in 'Duties of the Heart' teaches that our present is open to an evolution that will culminate in love.

"*The compassionate God wants the heart.*"[7]

We came to this world to love, and love is a tremendous force that carries us and protects us. To have a successful life, full of strength and confidence, we have to be successful in love. Rav Dessler teaches us, that to be able to love, one has to become a "giver."

---

[7] Sanhedrin 106b

5- Love is an immense force 2

What one person gives to another is an extension of himself, and it creates an attachment between two beings. It is an impulse of kindness that builds love. Our Creator, being the essence of goodness, wanted to create creatures to bestow this goodness on them. God wanted to donate GOOD, and that GOOD / *HATAVA*, be poured out on his creatures. God gives us many free gifts, but for humans to receive a more generous outpouring of GOOD, it must be through merit and not charity.

We are created in the image of God, so we have received surges of love to spread. Failure to diffuse these surges of love makes a man bitter and harsh and destroys his well-being. We must emulate this quality of 'giver' and offer others all the love we can give; this capacity must be strengthened throughout a lifetime. Rav Dessler teaches us that love and giving are linked. In a relationship, the one who doesn't give takes. He is a 'Taker." However, we all have the power to give because we have a divine spark within us, a part of the Great Universal Giver, God, our Creator.

Rav Dessler writes:

"If only we'd thought about it, we would realize that a person comes to love the one to whom they give. One would

come to realize that the only reason the other seems foreign to him is that he hasn't given him anything. He hasn't made an effort to show him a friendly interest. If I give to someone, I feel close to him; I have a part in his being. It turns out that if I were to spread the good to every person I come in contact with, I would very quickly feel that they are all my relatives, all my loved ones. I now have a part in all of them, for my being has expanded into each of them."

The same is true of love in a relationship. The one who gives loves. Couples break up, says Rav Dessler, because people generally prefer to be 'takers'; they outnumber the "givers."

"When the demands start, the love goes."

People who refuse to enter into marriage are unable to free themselves from the desire to take. This is why loving the other is a divine command, an order, an effort to be made, the control of his impulses. To love is a virtue.

"*I returned evil for good, and hatred is the price of my affection*," said King David. King David suffered from this destructive hatred, but he did not return hate for hatred. He asked his Creator to avenge him because the vengeance belongs only to God!

6- Love yourself

The first essential element to love others and to be successful in life is that you first have to love yourself.

"Love your neighbor as yourself"

It is written, "as yourself." A lot of people don't like themselves at all.

The person who lacks self-confidence and lacks self-love thinks that he is not what he wants to be, what he dreams of being. That person feels imperfect and can't stand it. She feels ashamed and shy or, on the contrary aggressive. She feels terrible about herself. Many feel the unexpressed desire to destroy themselves slowly; they smoke, take drugs, and have forbidden relationships or use violence, infidelity, ruin their health because they do not respect themselves. Within their being, a rejection of themselves is brewing, maturing, and torturing them.

"*Man must come out of his faults*," writes the Ramchal. We must, therefore, come out of our faults and not cry over them.

The fact that we are a creature of God and we are "his children" must give you a high opinion of who you are. Don't let your wrongdoing tarnish your outlook on yourself.[8] God created creatures who can make mistakes but also repair themselves.

We must overcome evil because man's goal is to repair himself on earth and mend the world through love. Sin is linked to unrepaired imperfection, so improving oneself is the action of fighting evil, says Ramchal.

If I don't love myself and criticize myself all the time, how can I love others and not blame them? If I only see the negative in myself and judge myself strictly, how can I see the positive in my neighbor? My brother, my enemy, is imperfect like me. He too "must come out of his faults."

---

[8] 'My Father, My King," Rav Pliskin

The image you have of yourself or of others is building or destroying you. If you are negative, it prevents you from using your potential and truly loving others.

Tell yourself that you are special in your Creator's eyes. We have infinite value because are his "child."

You have to say to yourself:

"I know I have to be special because God doesn't make worthless creatures."

Rabbi Pinhas of Koretz says:

"There is something precious in every being that cannot be found in anyone else."

7- Who is the mighty man?

"Who is the mighty man? The one who doesn't submit his inclination to evil. "[9]

Might is the ability to call upon one's inner strength to subdue one's evil inclination. Make it emerge, and there is greatness! Greatness knows how to get up every time you have fallen. For Judaism, the righteous is not the one who reached the top, but the one who knows how to make sustained efforts to get to it. Examine your soul, react after a failure to

---

[9] Ethics of the Fathers 4;1

continue progress towards elevation. This is the way to greatness.

"*If you won't be better tomorrow than you were today, then why do you need tomorrow?*" said Rabbi Nachman

Esau had a normal conduct until he was thirteen. Then, he let himself be attracted by the evil inclination. It tormented him from childhood, and even, as we are taught, in his mother's womb. Esau seemed to want to get out of it as soon as Rivka or Rebecca passed pagan places of worship. However, Esau had the potential to fight that attraction. His Creator had given him enough will and strength of character to control this temptation to evil. He had the free choice to choose his life.

Esau was a warrior by temperament, but he chose the wrong war, the fight against GOOD. He did not choose to fight evil. His brother, Jacob, on the contrary, had an attraction for GOOD. He hated to see evil reign around him. However, evil, wickedness, witchcraft came to attack him like little demons. He had to strive, as a man of the tents, to become a warrior who fought against these demons. The fight was not in his character. He'd must not deviate from the right path, and not fall from his greatness. Yet, he couldn't always be perfect. He had to obey his mother, Rebecca, who ordered him to impersonate his brother, Esau, to obtain the elder's blessing. Jacob loved the truth and did not want to cheat on his father or his brother. At that time, he was still a "man of the tents," with a good but reserved temperament. At the end of his life, he knew how to repel evil with vigor and live to reach the real good. He had filled his weaknesses. Esau, on the other hand, only reinforced his faults and his cruelty. Still, he had goodness in him. Esau loved and respected his father, Isaac.

Find out what your fight is! Don't let your past wrongdoings affect you. You can react and go up the hill. No one is completely bad, and evil is used to prove yourself.

8- Rabbi Meir Baal Haness

Rabbi Meir's true name was Nehorai. He was called Meir because he lit up the Halacha's wise men. He was part of the Great Tannaim (doctors of the Mishnah), of the fourth generation. He was a giant of his era. The mere mention of his name is known to perform miracles.

His undisputed master was Rabbi Akiba. Rabbi Meir was known for his lectures, and he used to divide them into three parts, a third of halakha, a third of stories, and a third of metaphors.

On the 12th of the month of Iyar - Second Passover - it is customary to visit the grave of Rabbi Meir and to donate *tzedakah*.[10] Although the exact date of his death is not known. Rabbi Meir promised salvation for all who give *tzedakah* to Israel's poor and for his soul's elevation.

Rabbi Meir was known in his generation for his power to solve any trouble, any need. Rabbi Meir is quoted as being one of the last five disciples who was left to Rabbi Akiba after the death of his 24,000 students.

It says in the Talmud that Rabbi Meir was descended from the Roman emperor Nero, who converted. Rabbi Yosi ben Halafta described him: "A great man, a holy man, a humble man."

---

[10] Charity

During the generation of Rabbi Meir, the Mishnah[11] was established and he held a central place in this edification. Rabbi Meir worked for a living as a Torah books and Megillot[12] scribe.

It is said in the Gemara[13] that one day he found himself in a place, on Purim, when there was no Meguilat- Esther that was kosher. He then began to write one, thanks to his phenomenal memory.

A Shabbat, while Rabbi Meir went to the synagogue, two of his children died. Bruria, his wife, said nothing to Rabbi Meir

---

[11] The **Mishnah** or **Mishna** (/ˈmɪʃnə/; Hebrew: מִשְׁנָה, "study by repetition", from the verb shanah שנה, or "to study and review", also "secondary") is the first major written collection of the Jewish oral traditions known as the Oral Torah. It is also the first major work of rabbinic literature (WIKIPEDIA)

[12] A scroll of the Book of Esther, read on the festival of Purim. 2. a scroll of the Book of Ruth, Song of Songs, Lamentations, or Ecclesiastes.

[13] Commentary on the Mishnah related to the Tanakh.

until the exit of Shabbat. She invented answers whenever he asked where his sons were. At the departure of Shabbat, she said:

"Someone left a deposit. This person comes back to claim his due, and it must be restored to him?"

And when Rabbi Meir replied affirmatively, she told him that his sons had died, and their souls lodged" on deposit "had been taken by the Creator. Thus, thanks to her courage and intelligence, Bruria allowed him to regain his senses and face the ordeal of losing his sons.

The Talmud tells some facts in which Rabbi Meir agreed to humble himself to bring peace in Jewish homes. So once, after an argument, a man demanded his wife to spit on Rabbi Meir's face. Rabbi Meir heard this, and decreed that he needed a woman to come to spit in his eye to exorcise the "evil eye." When the woman came to Rabbi Meir, he ordered her to spit in his eye seven times. When his disciples asked him why he accepted to be so humiliated, he replied: "*The honor of Meir is not larger than that of another* person," indicating that the humiliation was nothing compared to the loss of peace in a Jewish home, threatened by suspicion.

Rabbi Meir was nicknamed "Baal Haness," "The doer of miracles." This nickname was at the origin of a specific fact: Rabbi Meir went to save his sister in law captured by the Romans. When he tried to bribe one of the guards, putting his life in danger, he told the guard, "Only say, God of Meir, answer me!" and you'll be spared of punishment. The guard was convinced, and Rabbi Meir could save his sister-in-law, and whenever the guard was worried and in danger, he recited the words of Rabbi Meir. Each time he was saved; even when the emperor ordered that he'd be hanged, he used the words of Rabbi Meir, and the rope repeatedly broke until the execution was cancelled.

It is customary to tell the generations that Rabbi Meir asked to be buried standing up. He claimed that he would not expect the messiah sitting, but he would wait for him standing up.

9- We have the duty

We have the duty to know and understand that God is one, and to recognize that his Oneness is perfect:

"*Hear, Israel, the Lord is our God, the Lord is ONE.*"[14]

God is ONE means that:

Despite the existence of creatures, God is the only necessary existence, and that there is no other Creator.

---

[14] Deuteronomy 6;4

- That his power is unique and absolute. He rules the evil He created and the magicians:

"*God kills and gives life,*" Hana said in her prayer.

God alone rules the world: "*He has revealed you so that you may know ... There is none other than Him.*"[15]

The Sages of Israel added, "*Even witchcraft.*"[16]

The Unity of God alone is revealed to us. We must realize it, know it, and place it in our heart, without room for doubt:

---

[15] Deuteronomy 4 ; 35
[16] Sanhedrin 67;b

"In that day you will know and put in your heart that the Lord is God in heaven and on earth here below. There is no other."[17]

God is one / *yarid*. He is One, and He has no opposite. He is right, perfect; He is the supreme intelligence and the ultimate wisdom. He is generous and compassionate and has many other attributes as well.

The problem of deficiencies in the creation and that of evil are the will of God. According to God's perfection, he should only do good, but God created evil to oppose his revelation. It is up to us to reduce the evil to nothing to rediscover its Unity and make the ONE, which is veiled, shine again.

---

[17] Deuteronomy 4; 39

We are observing an imperfect and unjust world, and we might draw wrong conclusions. We have to do the job of proving that there is only goodness, fighting evil with a capital E. This struggle is called bringing back the Unity of God. The Unity of God is veiled and darkened until the evil is repelled. It is for man to oppose evil, and this must become his fight and his quest. The more we fight against evil, the more it is weakened and loses strength.

The perfection of the beginning of the universe at the time of its creation will be found at the end, as a train leaving its departure station would pass through the period of God's exile and return to the same station to complete its journey.

Perfection from the beginning will be found at the end.

Let us remember that God is the only existence necessary, the only power, the only governor, and that no one can do anything without the ok of God.

10- Life and death

Why do some people overcome life's trials and ultimately feel happiness and are uplifted, while others live poorly a life they see filled with failure and destructive suffering? It is because they made the wrong choice or no choice at all.

"I testify on you, on this day, heaven and earth: I have placed before you life and death, happiness and calamity; choose life! And then you and your posterity will live. "[18]

---

[18] Deuteronomy 30 ; 19

You cannot live every moment so that you feel peaceful and complete, without "choosing life." It is a choice that must be made on purpose; it is a choice that engages and it is a choice that requires vision. There are all kinds of visions: or living so that God will be proud of us and rejoice in his works. This is what we read in the morning prayer. For God to be proud, we must, for example, get out of our faults, work on our weaknesses, strengthen ourselves in *emouna*,[19] or even submit to the crises of life by deciding to overcome them.

- To choose life is also to choose a discipline for a productive life, study of Torah or Halacha, or any other enterprise of holiness.

---

[19] Faith and confidence in God

- To choose life is to do concerted actions of charity: to do free acts of kindness, to say encouraging words, to greet pleasantly anyone you meet, to greet people with a smiling face, etc.

A second choice is to let oneself be carried away by the events, good or bad, of our daily life. To remain passive and sad does not mean 'choosing life.' Imposing a demanding and perpetual life routine, such as metro, work, sleep with a lot of discipline, does not relate to 'choosing life,' but is to endure it. Choosing your ideals, your studies, cultivating yourself for own importance, working hard in order to be proud of your success does not correspond to the term "choosing life." "Choosing life" is a difficult choice. It is wanting a change of nature. It is wanting to move towards an evolution, towards a realization, towards the perfection of oneself, of others, and of the world.

The Ramchal tells us: "Creatures go through different periods during their lives, ascents and descents. These ascents and descents, all depend on God since he is the only essential Existence, the only Power, the only Governor of the world. These ascents and descents occur in the course of human evolution and development; to develop that is to say to repair oneself, do to *teshuva*, to realize oneself, to perfect oneself, to advance towards the completion of our being. A human being who never suffers great pain doesn't exist. However, it must not crumble, not despair, but rise and stand up.

"*Even if a righteous man falls seven times, he will rise, while the wicked collapse in misfortune.*"[20]

We must choose life and recover from difficult tests.

Ramchal in "Ways of Divine Direction" teaches: "Human tests, that us his trials, are placed in the crisis he has to overcome. Life gives us all kinds of pain and loss. Instead of asking, 'Why is it happening to me?' We must ask, even under the weight of immense pain, "What is the lesson from this situation? What do I learn from this test? How do I change,

---

[20] Solomon Proverbs Salomon 24:16

develop myself, and grow? Before every misfortune, one should say, 'God sent me a test in order to achieve my personal repair.'

11- The importance of a smile

Here are some anonymous proverbs that reflect the importance of smiling:

Be the reason someone is smiling today.

A good smile is still what dries the tears best.

Smiling is the shortest distance between two people.

Flowers need sun, humans need to smile.

Love is smiling, not with the mouth, but with the heart.

A face needs a smile to better communicate its beauty.

Every time a person smiles, they add something to their life.

Smiling makes friendships longer and families happier.

Smile when you answer the phone, the person on the phone will feel it.

To smile is to be ten years younger; to be sad is to make your hair gray.

You were in pain and a friend's mute smile comforted you. Do the same for others.

Make your smile change the world, not make the world change your smile.

You offered your smile to everyone. You filled our days with indescribable joy.

A smile creates happiness in the home, encourages goodwill in business and seals friendships.

It makes children's learning easier: when a parent or educator smiles, the child learns better.

Every smile you give someone changes their present and maybe their future as well.

The smiling person will be described as nicer, more sociable and even more competent than a person who is not smiling.

12- The purification of the act

I found it interesting to understand what is meant by 'the purification of the act.' This teaching is found in the Ramchal, 'Messilat Yesharim,' 'The Way of the Righteous,' and even before in the 'Duties of the Heart' by Baya ibn Pakuda. It is with this last text that I will shed light on this concept of purity of the act.

Baya ibn Pakuda, was a great master of the early Middle Ages. He taught us that man's worst enemy is passion, which in fact is nothing other than what we call *yeter hara* or evil inclination. It actually attacks man's reason because reason, the source of wisdom, can destroy this passion. Passion encompasses all uncontrolled emotions. Incidentally, *"The brain must control the heart."*[21] The passions are the need for fame, success, money, possessions; I would even say crazy love etc. The uncontrolled passion leads man into terrible doubt about the Truth with a capital T, the EMET in Hebrew; for example: all kinds of heresies, modern idolatry of games, cars, alcohol, drugs, and the path to the annihilation of our identity.

"Do not move the ancient landmark of your Fathers."[22]

"God asks for the heart."[23] So once we have acquired the wisdom to follow our Father's truth and their minds, and serve

---

[21] Sefer Tanya
[22] Solomon's Proverbs
[23] Sanhedrin 106b

God with our hearts, then it is good to turn to men. Ibn Pakuda taught us that our happiness or misfortune depends on them alone.

"*Your fate, mazal, is in their hands. Strive therefore to win their sympathy, find favor in their eyes;*" for the Masters of Israel said, "*He who pleases his fellow men pleases God. But he who does not please his neighbor does not please God.*"[24]

One can retort, writes Ibn Pakuda, that men are weak, unreliable; they are just a passing breath, and they already have trouble in their own family. And he continues: "*The man who is accepted, congratulated, praised by all, gives living proof that God has put his love in the soul*

---

[24] Ethics of the Fathers 3 ; 10

of each one because he does not do it for his enemies, but only for those whom he likes. But the wise man must not fall into the trap of flattery, and the beloved must answer within himself: What profit can I derive from honor and glory, I only know the extent of my duties towards God. "[25]

We can also retort 'My happiness is in my hands.' This is true if a man prepares to win the sympathy of his neighbor. It's a spread of love that will have its return.

And man must keep this precarious balance, like one who walks on a wire."

"If I'm not for myself who will be? And if I am for myself who am I? "[26]

---

[25] Duties of the Heart
[26] Ethics of the Fathers

13- A magnificent story

I discovered a wonderful story posted on the internet:

"One day a rich man gave a basket full of garbage to a poor man. The poor man smiled at him and left with the basket. He emptied it and cleaned it and then filled it with beautiful flowers. He went back to the rich man and gave him back the basket. The rich man was surprised and said to him: Why did you give me this basket full of beautiful flowers when I gave you garbage ? And the poor man said to him: "Each person gives what he has in his heart."

The one who knows how to love succeeds in his life, even if he is poor. Loving is the essential business of every day, a goal for each of us that requires daily effort.

14- Love ensures man's steps

"The whole world is a very narrow bridge, the main thing is not to give in to fear," said Rabbi Nachman of Breslev.

We overcome fear by attaching ourselves to the essential, which is love.

"Love thy neighbor!" our Creator commands us. Love is the rope that God tells us to grab to hold us together. All of his commandments are related to love; love and respect for others; not to offend them, not to steal them, not to envy them in an unhealthy way, not to harm them, not to lie to them, not to kill them, etc.,

Thornton Wilder, an American writer wrote this magnificent sentence:

"The bridge of love connects one to another, and gives dignity and purpose to even the lowest lives."

We came to this world to love, and love is an immense force that holds us up and protects us from the fall of the 'narrow bridge.' To have a life filled with meaning, you have to be successful, not in our career, not when acquiring goods and riches, but to succeed in loving.

15- We are one side

In the book "The Rebbe," by Joseph Telushkin we learn that the Rebbe[27] advocated contact with non-Jews to bring them to the realization that God is ONE. After clashes in Crown Heights,[28] where an African-American child was killed by a Jew in a car crash, the Rebbe expressed to Mayor Dinkins, also African-American, the hope that peace come back to town. Dinkins replied, "In both sides." The Rebbe continued, *"We are not two sides, we are one side. We are a people, living in a city*

---

[27] Rabbi Menachem Mendel Shneerson
[28] The New York's Chabad neighborhood

under an administration and under a God. May God protect the police and all the people of this city."

The Rebbe has said on different occasions: *"There are many of us but we are ONE; In God we trust."*

Here is a passage from one of my children's books: "Eli Solves the Riddle of God." This is the story of a marathon runner. When he wins the competition, his legs tell him:

- Reward us, your legs, because it is thanks to us that you won the competition.

- No! replicated the arms to the legs. We signed your entry into the competition and without our pendulum swing, he couldn't have run fast enough.

- And we, say the feet, we took a hit with every stride. Without us, sure he couldn't have run.

- You forget me, said the heart, without my accelerated beats nothing would have happened.

- And personally, adds the brain, I triggered and coordinated everything!

So spoke in turn every limb and organ of the athlete's body.

- So, who is right? they all asked.

-Personally, I say the brain! Estelle answers, because he controls everything.

- I say the heart, because without a beating heart, nothing happens! Ezra said.

- All are right! said Eli. One cannot without the other. They each have their own logic, and it is true. Every member tof the body is right. All members need to accept this and ask for a common reward in our little story *of the marathon runner. Among the proud, no one wants to accept the truth of the other, because it is not his truth. Differences of opinion lead to conflicts, violence, and wars. King David wrote in his Psalms that "the way of the wicked leads to ruin." Ruin means strife, violence and war.*

- I get it! The bad guys are those who refuse to listen to the opinions of others and want to uphold their law, said Ezra, cheeks flushed with excitement.

The Ramchal teaches:

"Man has the mission, to reverse Evil."

Evil is violence, argument, hatred and separation. To make Evil regress is to make peace reign at home, in one's family, with one's neighbors, and if one has stature, in one's country and in the world.

King David said:

"*The Lord protects the way of the righteous.*"

The Righteous are those who want to uphold Torah truth, law, security, justice and peace.

16- From evil comes good

"I trust in the Lord, I am not afraid. What man could do to me? "[29]

I wanted to study this concept of trust in God, and understand how even if a man hurts someone, good comes out of evil.

"When the Creator prepares good for man or for the world, it is always according to a very deep plan; which therefore first produces suffering."[30]

---

[29] Psalm 56 ; 12

[30] Ramchal in Daat Tevounot, pg 309

Also Torah, Israel, and the World to Come are acquired through suffering.

Jacob complained to his sons:
- Why did you hurt me?
The Creator replied:
- I am busy making his son reign in Egypt and he says why have you hurt me?

Likewise, David suffered. He was rejected by his family and sent to the pasture. He was not even present when the prophet Samuel came to anoint the future king in the family of Jesse / *Yshaï*. In the pastures David learned to use a slingshot to kill wild animals that threatened his flock. He killed lions and bears, so killing Goliath didn't scare him. The evil brought to him came to be good at the end.

Here is a little story [that I did not invent,] but that I report to image our subject:

It's just like that!

This is the story of an old farmer, who had three beautiful horses. He kept them in an enclosure at night. One morning the horses were gone. His neighbors told him: "What a bad luck my friend!"

The old farmer replied,

"It's not bad luck, it's just like that!"

The farmer's son who heard the misfortune occurred to his father came to visit him. He had gone to live in town because the countryside, he thought, did not have enough attractions compared to places full of animation like cities. On the way, robbers attacked the diligence in which he travelled, and the farmer's son was seriously wounded. He lost the use of his legs.

"What bad luck my friend!" the neighbors exclaimed.

The old farmer replied, "It's not bad luck, it's just like that!"

One morning, the farmer got up to wash his son and prepare him to drink when he saw that the horses were back to the enclosure.

"How lucky!" the neighbors exclaimed.

The old farmer replied, "It isn't luck, it's just like that!"

One day the war broke out. The strong and healthy neighbors' sons were called, to go to war for the king. The army refused to include the old farmer's son who was disabled.

"How lucky you are!" the neighbors exclaimed.

The old farmer replied, "It isn't luck, it's just like that!"

The war ended, and the neighbors' sons did not return. The old farmer ended his days with his son, and they took care of each other mutually. The son rode horses every day despite his disability, and this brought him great joy.

"How lucky you still have your son!" the neighbors exclaimed.

The old farmer replied, "Nothing is good luck or bad luck; all is well, it's just like that!"

17- Five Heresies

"Hear, Israel, the Lord is our God, the Lord is ONE."

In *'Daat Tevounot,'* the Ramchal teaches that certain conceptions about God's unity are false. These are five heresies:

1- Idolatry

The idolaters claimed that God is too high for humans and that he is not looking at them. They also claim that there were other gods below him to control the world. Therefore, idolaters served them and built altars where they offered sacrifices and incenses to attract protection. This heresy prevailed in Babylonia.

According to Judaism, the faith and trust in God require the recognition that only God dominates everything.

2- The two powers

These heretics claimed that there are two authorities; one that generates good and the other that generate evil. They thought that nothing exists without its opposite. It was the ancient tradition of Persian Zoroastrianism.

According to Judaism, the faith and trust in God require the recognition that God is the only Creator, and that he created good and evil:

"He forms the light and creates darkness, makes peace, and creates evil, I am the Lord who did all this."[31]

3- Nature

The third heresy claimed that the world follows the laws of nature. Work and zeal produce a positive influence, while laziness produces the opposite:

"My power and the strength of my hand have made this power then."[32]

Others say that everything depends on the Stars. Both views are similar. They were issued by the Greeks.

According to Judaism, the faith and trust in God require recognition that the One God has no second, no assistant, to run the world as advocated idolatry. All

---

[31] Isaïe 45; 7
[32] Deuteronomy 8;17

proceeds of his will alone, and not by chance, nature, or stars. The Creator controls each of his creatures individually.

4- Rejection Israel

Non-Jews consider that Israel has sinned and that instead of remaining right and fair, Israel has deviated from the chosen path and no longer deserve the divine benefits. They rely on this verse:

"*You have weakened the rock of your birth.*"[33]

According to Judaism, the faith and trust in God require recognition that the One God governs the whole earth and all it contains in the upper and lower spheres. If the Master of the World wants, he makes his actions depend on men's actions; and

---

[33] Deuteronomy 32; 18

when he wants, he does not consider the men's actions:

"I give thanks to whom I give thanks, even if he does not deserve it."[34]

"I will erase your sins to me, and I will remember more of your faults."[35]

5- The rebellion of Israel

Sinners among Israel rebelled against God and countered him just for pleasure like Amon:

"My only intention is to anger my Creator."[36]

Others believed that they could control things as they pleased with magic or witchcraft.

---

[34] Berakhot 7a

[35] Ibid 43; 25

[36] Sanhedrin 103b

Amon of Judah was the fifteenth king of Judah who succeeded his father Manasseh. Amon is best known for his idolatrous practices while he was king, which led to a revolt against him and ultimately his assassination.[37] His son Josiah succeeded him.

According to Judaism, faith and trust in God require the recognition that the One God is the Master of All, and that there is no other than Him.

The answer to these five points is what we have to believe. These five points constitute faith.

---

[37] Died in 641 BC

18- The Ramchal

The Ramchal, in 'The Way of the Righteous,' outlines the principle of "man's commitment to the world," *Chovat haadam be olamo*." Man must engage in a project of world arrangement, according to his talents.

"*To maintain one's engagement in the world is to act for the world's repair.*"

Man must make a commitment to improve the lot of the community in an absolutely selfless way.

God gives everyone the means to do their part in the world arrangement. These are strengths, and qualities and talents received from Heaven to fulfill one's social role. For each soul the arrangement of Creation takes a particular path depending on the purpose for which he was created. Each being has one or more roles and one or more missions. The talents, strengths and qualities that each one receives from Heaven must be used to fulfill his roles. King David had to be a fighter first. He recognized that God taught him the art of war.

"[The Lord] He instructs my hands in battle, my arm to wield the brass bow."[38]

David also acknowledged having received strength and physical ease:

---

[38] Psalm 18 ; 35

"... Supported by Him, I attack a battalion. ... You ease my steps and keep my heels from tottering ... It was you who armed me with valor for war, who made my aggressors bend. "[39]

Sometimes several talents are essential to a certain man's personality and his secondary roles. Thanks to his talents, David received the role of warrior. David also played other roles; through his artistic talent, music and literary composition, David also became the Gentle Singer of Israel, and he wrote the Psalms. David had of course the prominent role of king. His mission was to bring peace to the land; that is why there was peace in the days of his son, King Solomon.

---

[39] Psalm 18; 47

God helped David and Jeremiah to fulfill their mission by empowering them to fulfill it. God knew that David was going to be sharp and bloody, and Jeremiah was going to be fearful. Their first job was to get to know each other, and then to control their weaknesses, in order to be able to accomplish their roles and missions.

Even beings without a grandiose or historical destiny, simple people, each have their role to play and their destiny to achieve. They can and should illuminate their surroundings.

"You were created, like all of us, to oppose the hopes and views of the evil personified."[40]

---

[40] Book of Esther

So we have to purify our soul, and the Ramchal gives us the stages in "Messilat Yesharim," or "The Way of the Righteous," in order to oppose evil, and to illuminate our environment.

19 - Everything will be fine

Get into the habit of saying that 'everything will be fine' to be successful in your life. Encourage others and tell them 'everything will be fine.' Speech is creative. Wasn't the world created with ten words?

Words of encouragement can really give someone courage. *Emouna* / faith teaches us that nothing exists but God. Everything is holiness, and that God diffuses his good in ways often hidden behind an evil. However, the bitterness felt during the ordeal veils God's trust for those who suffer. Doubt is the evil inclination; it looks forward to getting into people's minds. It is the Garden of Eden's snake. When a person sees the glass half empty, he punishes himself.

Rabbi Nachman teaches that our problems turn into triumph if we do not go to war with God, but if we see our problems as tests to be overcome, and passed.

The word force and the thought which directs the word has the power to accomplish good. By being positive you receive the help of God. There is no point in worrying. Worry prevents one from accomplishing, and from solving difficulties; it creates anxiety and illness. Always think that 'everything will be fine.' *"Happy is he who puts his trust in God."*

"*Accept the will of God, for God to accept your will.*" [41]

God is the only will. You have to accept your trials by saying, 'with God's help, everything will be fine!'

---

[41] Avot, ch 2

20- Disunity

There is nothing more harmful to our people than disunity. Each of us must seek peace within the people, their family or couple, or those around us to create this union so desired by God.

Bad words create disunity, even if they never reach the ears of the subject of slander.

"Haim ve mavete be ad halashon; Life and death depend on words."[42]

---

[42] Hazal

Indeed, Rabbi Haim vital writes that the breath and the word are part of our soul. When we pass away, the soul leaves the body and takes with it the breath and the word, but the bad words we have said about others have made us lose part of our shining soul.

Rav Avraham Azoulai teaches that every word creates an angel, good, useless, or bad. These angels will be present when we'll sit before the Great Heavenly Tribunal. So, watching over his words is an act of wisdom. To say, for example, that our neighbor looks shabby, or that he is as big as a potato, that is slander. If the man is not careful in his words, it can be said that he is lacking in judgment. It is written in the Sifri on backbiting:

"*Cursed whoever strikes his neighbor in the shadows.*"

"*Who is the man who wishes for life ... save your tongue from evil.*"[43]

---

[43] Psalm 34; 12-13

21- Human speech

Human speech can be divided into four categories:

1) Bad words, backbiting in the shadows, malicious and dangerous words.

2) The second category is good and bad; that is: when two people are talking, and one person compliments a third one, his interlocutors may be bad or weak, or without self-esteem. So this can create jealousy, gratuitous hatred, and harm can follow. For example: "I heard X talking good things about Y. Ah! If she knew this or that, she wouldn't say too much about him/her. These words, originally good, can create evil at the same time.

3) The third category is speaking in vain. It's talking about everything and nothing, like weather, events, etc. It's neither good nor bad, it's in vain because it doesn't change anything.

4) The fourth category is absolutely good words. It is the words of Torah, the commandments and their observances, prayer and the Psalms, how to acquire good midotes or character traits, and to avoid bad ones, and how to improve one's way of being and one's life.

In summary, the wise conclude that the first two categories of speech are dangerous for others, but especially for us. The third is useless and without good results, as the number of words to be emitted is calculated for each one before is was born. The fourth category is words loved by God.

Maimonides adds a fifth category, permitted words; those useful for his personal life, business, and everyday life.

22- The *Emet* gives life

Solomon's proverbs teach:

"*Life and death depend on the word.*"

Our speech determine our spiritual life or death.

Rav Shalom Arush warns us[44] that that the obsessive desire to fill oneself with food and, on the contrary, satiety are also dependent on speech. Rav Arush tells us that the act of eating is in essence a spiritual act, and that eating right, healthy, denotes a holy spirit. He reminds us that

[44] In his book on the wisdom of women

the great sages were satisfied with a minimum amount of food and ate it slowly. They were considered alive, spiritually alive.

So the obsessive desire to fill oneself up represents a spiritual lack. Besides, to be healthy without illness and without being fed by anger or nerves denotes an active spiritual life. The two situations, obsession with food and satiety, also depend on speech.

Rav Arush adds that Rabbi Nachman[45] teaches that when a person prays, he is connected to EMET, to life, and derives vitality from it. Do not we say Torat-Emet, the Torah is life, and it contains the duty to praise God; praise is prayer. However, a person who routinely

---

[45] Likutei Moharan 1 ; 9

prays without putting his heart into it, Rav Arush writes that his prayers are considered to be lies. If you don't say, 'I will do this or that,' in addition to *Be Ezrat Hashem, with God's help*, it becomes a lie because you cannot do anything alone.

"He who is a deceiver will not dwell in my house; he who speaks a lie will not stand before my eyes."[46]

So we must strive to correct our words, for words which are not EMET, Divine Truth, are considered to be lies, and destroy us spiritually. This destruction takes away our soul's vitality, and by extension our body's vitality, for the soul animates the body.

---

[46] Psalm 101 ; 7

23- Abandoned to God

The one abandoned to God, is one who is filled with faith.

The prophet Habakkuk said: "*Tzaddik be Emounato y'hieh,*" "The Tsadik, his faith makes him live."

The tsaddik or the Just, is filled with inner peace and worries little about the things in his life. However, he is required to do his *hishtadlut,* that is, the effort to obtain what is necessary for his life; only the necessary and not the superfluous. For the superfluous, God can pour it out to him if he wishes.

The Tsadik should never think that:

"Those are my strength, my intelligence and my hands that have acquired all of this for me."

The following words are taken from the book "The Duties of the Heart," by Rabbi Bahiya ibn Pakuda. I quote in the chapter 'Shaar Habitachon,' translated Abandonment to God, 'by André Chouraqui:

"The abandoned one is satisfied with his lot and happy with what God gives him. Suffering exists for the abandoned one, but he knows that he is suffering to atone for his sins for eternal compensation. Abandonment lessens the suffering that arises from misery." I will translate misery as anxiety, depression, and despair, even anger.

I continue to quote:

"*Abandonment to God finally gives joy in all situations in which it pleases God to place man, even if they are contrary to his natural inclination. This is because of the refusal to accept life's problems as hardships to be overcome. Even more, we must want to illuminate our life with light, love of God, when evil confronts us. This light makes evil flinch because then God comes to our aid. It softens the decrees, the judgments against us and shortens the time of our suffering.*"

"*Hallelujah, Happy is he who reveres the Lord ... Light that shines in the shadows for the upright; He is merciful,*

merciful and just."[47] And God said, "*I glorify those who give glory to me.*" [48]

In these times of sadness, let us continue to glorify God, for the world is not ours.

---

[47] Psalm 112

[48] Samuel 1, ch2

24- The purpose of man's coming

The purpose of man's coming into the world, according to the Ramchal, noted in '*Shomer Emounim,*'and reported in '*Ner le Ragli,*' is to discover the *Emet*. The only truth. It is understanding that the Divine is everywhere and in everything: "*Immale kol haaretz cavodo.*' '*He fills the whole earth with his glory.*"

Man's job is to recognize this fact and to tear out the false belief that things or events happen by chance or by nature. Man must, therefore, struggle every day to extract these misconceptions from his thinking. Chance does not exist although our eyes and senses lead us to believe it. The *Emet* is invisible. Everything is Providence; it is God's will.

"*Ein od mi levado. There is nothing other than God.* "

A man's salary therefore depends on his chosen path, his works, and his ability to break the screen preventing to see that everything is *hashgara*, everything is divine. The effort that this work asks of us is very valuable because it helps us achieve our personal reparation, that of the world, the *tikun olam*, and our practical mission to move society forward. Good deeds help breaking the dark screen of our vision. This dark screen prevents us from seeing that God created the world and that He is managing the world and its rulers.

Didn't God harden Pharaoh's heart? Did not God bring the Hebrews to the land of Israel despite the spies' false report; did not God save Joseph from death to make him a king? Did he not reveal the future of Israel to the prophets? There are of course hundreds of other examples, which prove that God is ruling the world and history.

So let us remember that all the moments devoted to God: thoughts, words, prayers, studies, will be counted. Let us remember that the *Emet* is the divine will in our private lives, or in our history, and that of the world. Let's accept that everything is *hashgara*, everything is fair, and everything is for our good, and that of Israel.

25- God influences the Good

In 'Daat Tevounot,*[49] the Ramchal teaches us that God influences the Good which is His deep nature. However, evil is a creation of God. It is the veil that covers Good, the screen that cuts Good from the world. God created this screen because he wanted a world where the task of man would be to break this screen to release His divine light, and to repair himself.

"*I make peace and create evil,*" Isaiah [50]reports, that is, I created the

---

[49] Page 205
[50] [50] Isaiah 45 ; 7

screen of evil. It is written: *"He creates evil, but does not do evil."* He created it but does not diffuse it. We let it spread.

In a book for teens that I wrote, "Eli Solves the Riddle of God," it says:
"- You are free to choose evil. It you do, too bad for you! When the Good goes away, like a beautiful released balloon that flies up to the sky, then the sewer rats take up residence in your life. You will have opened the door for them."

Evil is released like rats escaping the sewers when we let it come into our lives.

As a result, God reduces the flow of Good.

"You have hidden your face and they are terrified,"[51] or again; *"I will hide My Face from them and they will be consumed."*[52]

However, there are times when God wants to disseminate his Good unconditionally, for example like those years in the desert where the people enjoyed divine protection. In other times, it is we who reinforce this occultation of the Good. Man sometimes does not do evil, but does not care to overcome his weaknesses. Jeremiah, the prophet, was fearful, and he was afraid to carry out his mission. The only possibility for him was to overcome his fear. Jacob was not combative enough to survive with Laban, he was a man of the study tents. He had to

---

[51] Psalm 104 ; 29
[52] Deuteronomy 31 ; 17

become a strong man so as not to lose his holiness and fight the angel of evil. He has made up his shortcomings to accomplish his mission.

Depending on our conduct as a people and as an individual, the divine flow is sometimes reduced. When the divine flow is delivered in abundance it would be like a healthy body. When the flow is partially delivered, the evils are declared in proportions of this body. When the flow stops, the body dies. Each day that God gives us brings with him the opportunity to do good.

Age, loneliness, suffering should not prevent us from breaking this dark screen of evil. We must change our minds and tell God that we accept this suffering since it is of course for our repair; and this acceptance is returning to God out of love.

26- Good luck and bad luck

THE RASHA

Definition: the r*asha* is the one who denies the thirteen principles of the faith stated by the Rambam, the *sloch essre ikarim*. This is what we call an *apikorsus*. He loses the merit of the Fathers.

Man's interiority must be good and he must perfect himself to gain entry into the Other World, the *Olam Haba*. The *rasha* is not interested in *Olam Haba*. He wants this world. It is Eisav personified, Esau in English. He therefore becomes bad because nothing prevents him from acting according to his desire since he is not afraid of Heaven.

The *ben sorer or moré* is the rebel. He rebels against God and, therefore, against his parents. His potential is bad. God created the *reshaim*, the bad ones for the days of misfortune. However, they inherited the possibility of coming back to God. The *rasha* has the choice to transform his potential by making an effort to serve God, and by doing social work. Everyone is redeemable except for the Amalek's offspring.

Why the Rasha et tov lo? Why the heretic that we also call the evil one, the ungodly, everything smiles at him, why is he lucky?

The bad ones are indifferent to God, they live their lives doing only what pleases them. They do not think that the trials are punishments, but the work of bad luck. They acquire a lot of good things, but those good things are in fact nuisances. They are like cancers that devour them because of all the harmful consequences that they bring with them. For example, a man who embezzles money does so without remorse because he thinks that Heaven is not interested in men's affairs. He buys a large property, but will not have the leisure to live happily in it for long. The *rasha* receives his reward for his good deeds in this world.

The *rasha* sometimes does good deeds, but they are for his sake, either for glory or to get something in return. So this is what the *rasha* receives as wages in this world, *Osher ve Kavod*, honor and contentment.

Sometimes, nothing is going well for the *rasha*. This is when Hashem shakes him with hardship to try to save him and awaken him to teshuva. The situation of the "*rasha ve ra lo*," to whom difficult trials come, this one is in a better situation than the *rasha* that God allows to be destroyed with the good things which lead to his destruction.

The good deeds done for the glory of Heaven, come from the desire to do the will of God; and having the Other World is a lower level than wanting to do the will of God purely and simply. These good deeds also receive honor and contentment; this is their salary in this world, but in addition, they receive an extension of days, which is the Next World.

27- Two funerals

This is the story of two Jews who died on the same day.

There was a bad Jew in a simple wooden coffin, and there was no one to accompany him. Next to him, was an honorable Jew with a large crowd coming to pay him homage, in a solid wooden coffin. They were to be buried in the cemetery of *Har HaZetim*.

Young Arabs arrived screaming and throwing stones. The frightened crowd of Jews fled, laying the two coffins on the ground.

These pious people got their act together, and they came back soon after, to finish the funerals. They, therefore, proceeded to the burials. However, it happened that the Arabs, for having fun, had moved the bodies. They put the bad Jew in the beautiful coffin and the rich man in the simple wooden coffin.

That same night, the Rabbi who carried out the burials had a dream. From Heaven, they sent him the information about the error. La *Hevra Kadisha,* les Jewish funeral pumps decided to check the problem by opening the two coffins. It was true! The Rabbi was appalled.

The following night, the rich man came to him in a dream and said to him "It's all right! Because I made a serious mistake, I lost the right to an honorable homily, and this man who has done only one great deed in his life has been rewarded for it."

Esau was not interested in the Next World. He had his rewards in this world.

28- The quarrel

Everyone thinks that he has the truth on his side, teaches the Hafets Haïm. Each thinks that the other is responsible and deserves punishment. Each antagonist develops the desire to quarrel and to win. The result is the desecration of the name of God.

Rabbi Akiba's students, all Torah scholars, did not respect each other. They did not honor each other, and they died as a result, because they profaned the Divine Name. They each felt that the disrespect fell on the other and not on himself. All of their Torah knowledge and holiness did not protect them from the punishment and attribute of righteousness that hit them hard.

Even if a man is right and his opponent is punished because of him, the one who is right will end up being punished too.

God said to David:

"Because of you, the priests of Nov were killed, and Doeg lost his Olam Haba."

Although David was allowed to defend himself, he was nonetheless punished and endured great suffering. Why?

"It is forbidden to belittle one's neighbor."

Woe to this joy, and woe to the joy of rejoicing in the fate of the punished. The dignity of the punished must be preserved.

Take the story of Avihu and Jeroboam for example: Jeroboam was apparently at fault in an argument. God struck him with a plague, and he died. Avihu lost his strength because he rejoiced over Jeroboam's fate, and he could never do anything again.

29- With fear comes the fall

"When you go out and fight against your enemies, [Moses said to the Hebrew people,] and see horses and chariots - and forces greater than yours, do not be afraid of them, for the Lord your God, who brought out of the land of Egypt, will be with you. … When you are about to fight, the priest must come forward and He must say to them: "Shema, Israel! Listen, O Israel! You are about to give battle to your enemy. Don't let your courage weaken. Do not be afraid or panicked or in fear of the enemy, for the Lord your God who walks with you will obtain victory for you. "

This commandment to be courageous is based on the *mitzvah of bitachon be Hashem. It is* the duty to have complete confidence in God's Providence over our lives. It is valid at all times of fear.

Fear is intrinsic to humans. As soon as Adam and Eve sinned, they were afraid. Only a man who is without sin would avoid knowing fear. Fear is a feeling that weakens a being. It is why, repeatedly, in the events recounted in the Torah, God asks his creatures, "*Do not be afraid, or do not fear.*"

God reassures Abraham with promises of protection for him and his descendants. Hagar, who became, according to the *Midrash*, Abraham's wife after Sarah's death, saw her son Ishmael dying of thirst. An angel of God cried out to her, "*Do not fear!*" and she discovered water.[53] When Jacob was preparing for his trip to Egypt, to find his son Joseph after twenty years of separation, God gave him courage because he did not want to leave the Promised Land.

The prophets also repeated God's words to us:

"Do not be afraid, for I am with you. Do not be afraid, for I am your God. "

If we increase in trust in God, in the assurance that all is well and for our good, even the suffering that cleans up our faults, then our intrinsic fear will decrease step by step.

---

[53] Genesis 21:17

Maimonides sees the commandment *"not to be afraid"* as one of the 365 negative Torah commandments."

"With fear comes the fall."

30- To strengthen our trust in God

You have to be afraid of Hashem and nothing else.

When we wake up in the morning, we are often fearful: What will happen today? Is Iran going to hit us in revenge for Israel's supposed attacks on its sites, on Syrian territory? Will the Corona kill thousands of us? Or any other sad fear. So, you have to react and affirm to your Creator that you will live every moment of the day in joy:

"This is the day that God made, let us rejoice and be happy."[54]

We have to act like Shifrah and Pouah, in their frightening ordeal before Pharaoh. He [Pharaoh] thought that these women would be afraid of him and that they would do the dirty work of exterminating the male children for him. Now, this is what they say to each other before their meeting with Pharaoh [according to the Midrash]:

-   Abraham, our ancestor, did everything to apply the principle of charity and justice, said Yocheved, and we are going to kill each other? Better to risk death! God is stronger than Pharaoh. Pharaoh has his idea, but the God's idea

---

[54] Psalm said in the Halel

will prevail. It is He whom we must serve and glorify! He created the universe and he maintains it. Pharaoh is just one of his pretentious creatures.

- Well, we will strengthen our confidence in God and help the childbirth of our people, like Abraham, with charity and justice! I prefer to go in the way of Abraham and please God!

- My daughter, God bless you for saying that!

Haya Evelyne Berkowitz was born in Nice and raised in Marseille. After a long detour to the United States, she found her true roots in Jerusalem and also discovered spirituality. Today she transmits the wisdom of the great Masters of Israel through personal development stories and books.

She devotes herself to writing, painting, teaching and art therapy.

BILINGUAL BOOKS

LIVRES BILINGUES ET HISTOIRES BILINGUES sont des séries destinées aux étudiants d'une deuxième langue et ont un double objectif : la compréhension du texte et l'enrichissement du vocabulaire.

BILINGUAL BOOKS AND BILINGUAL STORIES are series aimed at students of a second language and have a dual purpose: understanding of the text and vocabulary enrichment.

N°1

Français- anglais avec texte parallèle-
Niveau Intermédiaire
French – English with parallel text-
Intermediate Level

3 Histoires Bilingues
3 Bilingual Stories

1 - Qu'en sera-t-il demain ?
What about tomorrow?
2 - L'appel du destin.
The Call of Destiny
3 - Un soudain éclair de lumière.
A Sudden Burst of Light

N∘2

Français- anglais avec texte parallèle- Niveau Intermédiaire

French – English with parallel text- Intermediate Level

3 Histoires Bilingues

3 Bilingual Stories

1 - Qui sauve une vie…

Whoever saves a Life…

2 - Le meilleur des étés

The Best of Summer

3 - Demain sera peut-être mon dernier jour

Tomorrow might be my last day

N∘3

Français- anglais avec texte parallèle-
Niveau Intermédiaire
French – English with parallel text-
Intermediate Level

3 Histoires Bilingues
3 Bilingual Stories

1 - Même le plus noir nuage
Even the darkest Cloud
2 –Un jugement de Salomon
A Judgment of Salomon
3 - Le carnet
The Notebook

N◦4

Niveau débutant -Beginner Level

Seul contre tous
Alone Against Them All

Nimrod est furieux. Sa figure est rouge comme une cerise mure.
Nemrod is furious. His face is as red as a ripe cherry.
- Tu te moques de moi ! Nous allons servir le feu et je vais te jeter dedans. Nous verrons si ton Dieu est plus fort que le mien !
- You are kidding me! We are going to serve the fire, and I am going to throw you into it. Let's see if your God is stronger than mine!

N∘5

3 EASY BILINGUAL STORIES

Conversational French Dialogue
with English parallel text

French – English – Advanced Beginner
Level

1 HISTOIRE BILINGUE – 1 BILINGUAL STORY

N°1

. La voleuse

. The Thief

Niveau avancé

Advanced Level

Pépin et Samuel sont en chemin pour rejoindre l'Empereur Charlemagne à Lyon. Durant une pause, ils font une rencontre étrange.

Pepin and Samuel are on their way to meet Emperor Charlemagne in Lyon. During a pause, they make a weird encounter.

N°2

. L'appel du destin
. The Call of Destiny

Niveau Débutant Supérieur
Upper Beginner level

David me répétait : « le Seigneur est bon et tu dois soumettre ta volonté à sa volonté, car si tu le fait, tu accompliras ton destin. «

So David kept telling me: « The Lord is good, and you need to submit your will to his will, for if you do, you will reach your destiny.»

N∘3

. Un soudain éclair de lumière

. A Sudden Burst of Light

Niveau intermédiaire

Intermediate Level

Eva a un gros problème personnel qu'elle ne peut pas résoudre. Ruth rentre dans sa vie.
Va-t-elle l'aider ou non?

Eva has a significant personal problem which she cannot solve. Ruth gets into her life.
Is she going to help her or not?

N°4

. Qu'en sera-t-il demain?

. What about Tomorrow?

Niveau intermédiaire

Intermediate Level

PEPITO GONZALES, un garçon de ferme, de quatorze ans, défie son ennemi, Rosita, de monter sur une colline hantée.
Que se passe-t-il là-bas ?
PEPITO GONZALES, a fourteen-year-old Mexican farm boy, dares his enemy, Rosita, to go up on a haunted hilltop.
What is going on there?

On sale on amazon.fr and amazon.com [E-book and print book]

FROM 6 YEARS OLD

- THE FIGHT AGAINST MALIFACE

CHILDREN BOOKS

- ABRAM'S CHOICE

- THE GREATNESS OF ISAAC

- JACOB'S STRENGTH

TEENS AND YOUNG ADULT BOOKS

- ELI RESOLVES GOD'S ENIGMA

- SOLOMON PROMISE. The Secret of the Hundred Doors

- A STRANGE CITY. The Secret of the Hundred Doors

- WHEN THINGS GO WRONG. The Secret of the Hundred Doors

- THE EVIL EYE. The Secret of the Hundred Doors

- ELI SOLVES GOD'S ENIGMA (Coming of age/Knowing God)

- MY JOURNEY BEYOND THE WALL

-DAVID THE CONQUEROR (Historical and Biblical)

- BEFORE IT IS TOO LATE (Historical and Biblical)

BOOKS IN ENGLISH

- HOW TO MAKE STUDENTS ENJOY LEARNING (with affective and creative teaching)

- THE FINAL OBJECTIVE (THE FINAL OBJECTIVE is a translation of the abridged version of: L'ECLAT MANQUANT DANS LE FIRMAMENT. A Biography of Rabbi Moses Chayim Luzzatto, known as the Ramchal, Cabbalist. 1707 – 1746.

-THE LAST BLUE DRESS (Historical-Memoir)

- BECAUSE I WANTED TO LIVE (Memory of a fourteen years old survivor, from the Nazi deportation, in France.)
- WHAT DOES THE ESSENCE OF JUDAISM TEACH US?

- THEY HAVE CHOSEN TO LIVE

- WHAT MAKES A WOMAN SHINE?

- SELF EXPLORATION with 60 exercises

- THE LIGHT SPRUNG FROM THE HOLE

- THE GUIDE TO GREATNESS: FIRST, LOVE YOURSELF

- THE GUIDE TO GREATNESS: CREATE JOY
- THE GUIDE TO GREATNESS: IT IS STILL TIME TO SPREAD LOVE